TRADING

STRATEGIES

A Practical Guide and Advanced Techniques in Trading to High Probability of profit.

(book 6 of 6)

BY Robert Davis

Introduction

The correct investment strategy can probably be the best pathway to independence from the rat race. Regardless of whether it fills in as an enhancement to your ordinary pay, extra reserve funds for retirement, or an approach to take care of obligation — the best investment procedures can affect your monetary wellbeing to improve things.

That being said, there are countless such sorts of investment systems that can appear to be overpowering from the start. From stocks and bonds to land, there are various alternatives accessible. The accompanying aide will cover a couple of amateur cordial investment procedures and help you track down an ideal choice for your circumstance and objectives. Continue to peruse to find out additional. Start by opening an IRA; at that point, grow your investments utilizing file assets and ETFs, and contribute close to 10% of your portfolio in organization stocks. For some Americans, a business-supported 401(k) is their first investment vehicle, with 65% of U.S. laborers offered one or a similar arrangement. Yet, to fabricate abundance, you additionally may need or have to contribute outside of that arrangement. The best thing about contributing procedures is that they're adaptable. On the off chance that you pick one and it doesn't precisely measure up for your danger resilience or timetable, you can make changes. Be that as it may be cautioned: doing so can be costly. Each buy conveys a charge. All the more critically, selling resources can make an acknowledged capital addition. These increases are available and, in this way, costly.

Here, we take a gander at four regular contributing techniques that suit most financial backers. By setting aside the effort to comprehend the attributes of every, you will be in an ideal situation to pick one that is ideal for you over the long haul without the need to bring about the cost of shifting direction. A typical fantasy about contributing is that multiple ledgers are required to begin. In actuality, the way toward building a solid portfolio can start with a couple thousand—or even two or three hundred—dollars.

This story offers explicit counsel, coordinated by the sum you may have access to start your investments. To begin with, be that as it may, it covers some shrewd moves low-rollers can make to launch a reserve fund and investment program. To start contributing, pick a strategy dependent on the sum you'll contribute, the courses of events for your investment objectives, and the measure of hazard that bodes well for you. Lease, service charges, obligation installments, and staple goods may seem like everything you can bear the cost of when you're simply beginning. Be that as it may, whenever you've dominated planning for those month-to-month costs (and put away, at any rate, a little money in a backup stash), it's an ideal opportunity to begin contributing. The exciting part is sorting out what to put resources into — and how much.

As an amateur to the universe of contributing, you'll have a lot of inquiries, not the least of which is: How would I begin, and what are the best investment techniques for fledgelings? Our guide will respond to those inquiries, and that's just the beginning.

Before you start to explore your investment strategy, it's critical to accumulate some fundamental data about your financial circumstance. Ask yourself these essential inquiries:

- What is your present financial circumstance?
- What is your typical cost for essential items, including month-to-month expenses and obligations?

- What amount would you be able to bear to contribute—both at first and on a continuous premise?

Even though you needn't bother with a great deal of money to begin, you shouldn't start on the off chance that you can't stand to do as such. On the off chance that you have many obligations or different commitments, consider the effect contributing will have on your circumstance before you begin setting money to the side.

Then, put out your objectives. Everybody has various necessities, so you ought to figure out what yours are. Is it true that you are proposing to put something aside for retirement? It is safe to say that you are hoping to make enormous buys like a home or vehicle later on? Or on the other hand, would you say you are putting something aside for your kids' schooling? This will help you restricted down a strategy.

Sort out what your danger resistance is. This is ordinarily controlled by a few key elements, including your age, pay, and how long you have until you resign. The more youthful you are, the more danger you can take on. More danger implies better yields, while lower hazard implies the increases will not be acknowledged as fast. However, remember, high-hazard investments likewise mean there's a more prominent potential for misfortunes also.

At long last, gain proficiency with the fundamentals. It's a smart thought to have a fundamental comprehension of what you're getting into so you're not contributing aimlessly. Pose inquiries. Furthermore, read on to find out about a portion of the vital methodologies out there.

Chapter 1: Value Investing

Worth financial backers are deal customers. They look for stocks they accept are underestimated. They search at stocks with costs they accept don't completely mirror the natural worth of the security. Worth contributing is predicated, partially, on the possibility that some level of mindlessness exists on the lookout. This silliness, in principle, presents freedoms to get a stock at a limited cost and bring in money from it.

It's excessive for esteem financial backers to search over volumes of financial information to discover bargains. A large number of significant worth common subsidizes allow financial backers the opportunity to claim a bushel of stocks thought to be underestimated. The Russell 1000 Value Index, for instance, is a famous benchmark for esteem financial backers and a few shared assets impersonate this record.

As examined above, financial backers can change techniques whenever however doing as such—particularly as a worth financial backer—can be expensive. Regardless of this, numerous financial backers abandon the strategy following a couple of poor-performing years. In 2014, Wall Street Journal correspondent Jason Zweig clarified, "Over the course of the decade finished December 31, esteem reserves gaining practical experience in huge stocks returned a normal of 6.7% yearly. However, the average financial backer in those assets acquired simply 5.5% annually."1 Why did this occur? Since such a large number of financial backers chose to haul their money out and run. The exercise here is that to make esteem contributing work, you should play the long game.

You most likely haven't considered purchasing a stock purchasing stock. Most Millennial financial backers don't. Examines have shown that Millennial financial backers are inactive in their investment strategy. You may, in general, support things like your 401(k) or file reserves due to their straightforwardness. However, this isn't generally the most thoughtful approach to contribute.

Worth contributing is clever contributing. I'll utilize the terms conversely in this article. Worth putting centres around putting resources into a quality organization that you believe is underestimated. You settle on this choice dependent on solid essential examination.

It's a purchase and-hold strategy. It focuses on market eruptions to recent developments and to which organizations deliver profits. This leaves a few organizations underestimated, dependent on their drawn-out development potential.

Benjamin Graham is the creator of The Intelligent Investor. In certain circles, he's known as the "Father of Value Investing."

He says that astute financial backers perform total and top to bottom investigations before contributing. Doing this will give them protected and consistent profits from their investments.

They centre around evaluating, as well. Savvy financial backers possibly purchase a stock when its cost is underneath its natural worth.

The characteristic worth is the way you esteem the organization dependent on your major investigation. You do this while disregarding the market. As such, I fail to remember what every other person is saying.

Keen financial backers additionally search for an edge of wellbeing before purchasing a stock. This implies you believe there's a hole between what you'll pay for the supply and what you'll acquire from the store as the organization develops.

To recap, esteem contributing spotlights on:

- Solid central investigation
- Finding and purchasing stocks that are underestimated
- Purchasing with an edge of security

The three principles of value investing

1. Do your exploration

Set aside some effort to dissect and comprehend the organization you are putting resources into before purchasing any stock. You ought to understand the accompanying things about the organization:

- its long-term plans
- it's business principles
- its financial structure
- the group that oversees it (the CEO, CFO, and so forth)

Worth contributing spots attention on organizations that deliver reliable profits. Why? Develop, productive organizations regularly take care of part of their benefits to their financial backers. This piece of the service is known as a profit.

Keen financial backers consistently look past an organization's momentary income also. They don't mind if the organization is well known in the media.

2. Enhance

At any point, hear the expression "don't tie up your resources in one place"? All things considered, it applies to esteem contributing, as well.

Shrewd financial backers have various kinds of investments in their portfolios. This shields them from genuine misfortunes. Even though worth contributing has been demonstrated to bring to the table consistent yearly returns, it's not ensured.

3. Search for protected and consistent (not phenomenal) returns

This one is generally difficult for new financial backers to get a handle on. Everybody needs to bring in money quick. For what reason do you think there are so many "5 Best Stocks for... " articles out there?

In school, I had a class called Advanced Investments. My educator consistently said that assuming you're finding out about a "hot stock," it's now past the point where it is possible to contribute. It bodes well. However, we get tied up with the promotion.

Not many of us need to invest the Momentum and exertion to get protected, consistent returns. We need stocks that will detonate in worth and give remarkable returns. That is not reasonable.

You could discover stocks like that, and it might even keep going for some time. Yet, it will not keep going forever. Sooner or later, that strategy will fizzle.

So as opposed to looking for quick, market-beating returns, clever financial backers need consistency. A canny financial backer will be content with generally safe, predictable profits from their investments after a seemingly endless amount of time after year.

Search for stocks that meet your necessities. Try not to attempt to beat the arrangement of the individuals who do this professionally.

Presently it's an ideal opportunity to begin in picking a few stocks. Be that as it may, where would it be a good idea for you to start?

To begin with, you'll need to decide whether you're a cautious financial backer or an ambitious financial backer.

It's typical of a cautious financial backer to:

- hope to diminish hazard as frequently as could be expected
- adopt a more inactive strategy to dealing with their portfolio
- enhance by putting resources into developing blue-chip stocks just as high-grade bonds

Ambitious financial backers are generally:

- more dynamic in dealing with their investments
- willing to face challenges on more current organizations in the desire for a better yield
- expanded, however, place a heavier load on stocks

There's no incorrect method to contribute. Both can be shrewd financial backers on the off chance that they keep the standards of significant worth contributing.

Whenever you've chosen how you need to contribute, it's an ideal opportunity to begin searching for stocks. While I don't propose you go out and purchase a store quickly, I comprehend your time is significant.

I utilize the Classic Benjamin Graham Stock Screener by Serenity Stocks. This is a phenomenal device to get you headed the correct way in searching for underestimated stocks.

When you discover a few stocks you like, start your examination. I was hoping you could make sure to look at the extra connections I've included after each part. This will help you review anything you're new to.

After you've done your exploration, it's an ideal opportunity to contribute. Make a point to contribute what you're open to losing. Keep in mind and there are no assurances in contributing—even worth contributing.

Foreign Investments: Why Should Take the Leap

Youthful grown-ups enjoy a benefit regarding contributing: Longtime skylines mean you can face more challenge than more seasoned individuals. On the off chance that you are alright with more severe dangers, unfamiliar business sectors are an extraordinary chance to get better yields.

Putting resources into unfamiliar business sectors can be somewhat confounding. They appear to be going here and there constantly, and large crashes worldwide continue to make the news. So for what reason would it be advisable for you to get included?

There are two primary reasons foreign assets will profit both your funds and your mental soundness. They can:

- Expand your investment portfolio
- Permit you to exploit the long haul development potential

Regardless of how developed, each market will go through a progression of ups, downs, and adjustments on a semi-standard premise. Purchasing stocks in unfamiliar business sectors that follow an alternate design than the US adds a layer of safety to your investment. It's simply savvy not to keep all your assets tied up in one place. The US has a developed routinely exchanged investment market. It pushes ahead at a moderately sluggish, consistent speed, which makes it harder to acknowledge enormous additions to your investments. Then again, unfamiliar business sectors, similar to the more youthful economies of Eastern Europe, South America, Africa, Asia, and the Middle East, have tremendous long haul development potential.

The keen method to make unfamiliar investments

Stock costs go here and there—it's precisely what they do. Markets will take short plunges, and economies will stumble into difficulty. This choppiness is imperative to follow on the off chance that you are a stock representative, and your responsibility is to make the present moment risky investments. In any case, when you are working for the future, it doesn't bode well to watch these everyday vacillations.

What are significant are the drawn-out patterns that are not influenced by transient market unpredictability. You care about your future—a stock going here and two or three pennies short-term shouldn't mean a lot to you contrasted with its pattern over numerous years.

ETFs and ease common assets are an excellent method to get the drawn-out advantages of foreign market investment while limiting the transient dangers.

Both work by gathering stocks and markets together. Rather than becoming tied up with a solitary organization that may fail spectacularly, you become tied up with a gathering of organizations that sell an assortment of items and administrations; the variety shields you from momentary misfortunes by engrossing any stun waves.

Most importantly, it's brilliant to get into ETFs or shared assets with low-cost proportions that are adequately different to cover a decent cross-part of the market. There a lot of alternatives to browse, including:

Vanguard Total International Stock ETF (VXUS)

This ETF covers the whole global market outside the US. That is comparably different (and protected) as you can get when contributing universally.

iShares MSCI Pacific ex-Japan (EPP)

This asset is more explicit, covering stocks just in Asia, however barring Japan. The developing business sectors of China and India could give critical development throughout the next few decades.

Vanguard European Stock Index Fund (VEURX)

Morningstar calls this asset "perhaps the most ideal choice for uninvolved openness to European stocks," a financial backer can discover. Even though Europe has encountered unpredictability this decade, that could mean you get the opportunity to purchase low and watch the business sectors settle and fill later on.

Any investment is at any rate somewhat dangerous. Yet, hazard is important to get any opportunity of gains. Unfamiliar business sectors are less secure than US markets, yet they additionally have a higher possibility of developing over the long haul.

Try not to get tricked by the news reports—market variances are characteristic, and make little difference to genuine development throughout extensive stretches of time. Placing the part of your investments in unfamiliar business sectors either through ETFs or ease common assets and playing the long game will augment your opportunity of genuine increases over your lifetime.

Understanding Your Mind Will Make You a Better Investor

You see how your psyche functions will help you improve investments. Find three ideas that clarify how you think — and how that can make you a superior financial backer.

Contributing without seeing how your mind is settling on choices is an exercise in futility. It's likewise a misuse of money.

This post will uncover a couple of influential ideas that will change how you consider contributing. Applying these ideas will make you a superior financial backer over the long haul.

My failed investment

At the point when I was more youthful, I settled on vast loads of incautious investment choices. Not simply with stocks. I thought it'd be an excellent investment to purchase Teenage Mutant Ninja Turtle activity figures in school. The statistics were as yet in their unique bundling. I figured I'd get them in mass, at that point, auction them individually for tremendous benefits. Good thought, isn't that so?

For reasons unknown, the market for purchasing toys wasn't as I'd anticipated. The more significant part of individuals purchasing figures on eBay were re-merchants like me, wanting to make a speedy buck. So no one was buying. I wound up losing money on the investment, having to exchange the vast majority of the figures in mass for a misfortune.

Thinking back on the investment, I realize it was dumb. It was rash. I didn't do any examination. It didn't bode well. So for what reason did I do it?

You've doubtlessly been in the present circumstance previously. You purchase a stock (or some other kind of investment), and it loses esteem. After you've assumed your misfortune and proceeded onward, you can't help thinking about why you made that investment in any case. Was it somebody's recommendation? Is it true that you were attracted to the organization's items? Did you think you were beating the market?

Nobel Prize champ Daniel Kahneman composed an incredible book called Thinking, Fast and Slow. The book examines the brain science behind how our psyche functions. The exploration in the book applies to contributing, also. We should investigate a portion of the ideas and understand they can make you a superior financial backer.

Concept one: Your two minds

Our brain has two frameworks that interact with data. It influences how we think, concoct choices, act, and judge circumstances. This is urgent when you're contributing. The first is framework one. I like to consider it our "sluggish mind." System 1 is the piece of the cerebrum that responds on instinct. It's hasty and programmed. It's non-cognizant.

For instance, you may purchase stock in an organization since they have a hot new item out. You think it'll change how purchasers carry on. You don't want to delve into the organization's financials or history immediately. Your framework one brain is attracted to the story and leads you to make an indiscreet, apathetic choice.

To clarify this somewhat further, I'll utilize the model from the book:

A bat and a ball cost $1.10. The bat costs a dollar more than the ball. What amount does the ball cost?

Without a doubt, you said a dime. This is your framework one working; however, it's mistaken. On the off chance that you pause for a minute to figure it out, you'll see that the appropriate response is five pennies. So what was the deal? Your framework one depended without really thinking to respond to the inquiry you thought was basic.

How should this influence your investment choices?

The following kind is framework two, and it's more cognizant. It requires exertion. It's the piece of our mind that will permit us to concentrate. We would then be able to make intentional, thought-out choices. Yet, it additionally necessitates that you put your motivations away and focus.

We should look again at the model above. If you're utilizing your framework two, you may settle on an alternate choice on the stock. You may prevent yourself from purchasing the store in the wake of dissecting the organization's financials. Or on the other hand, you may see they have numerous contenders and a little unreasonable net revenue.

My framework one was the essential driver of my investment in Ninja Turtles activity figures. I purchased the figures without much forethought. I disregarded the expenses. I missed the likely absence of benefit. This was supportive of the appeal of buying and selling toys from my youth.

Train your mind to be less passive and utilize your System two all the more frequently. By doing this, you'll increment the strength of your insight. You'll likewise turn out to be more engaged when you settle on investment choices.

Here are five phenomenal mind preparing applications for you to attempt at this moment:

- Elevate
- Lumosity
- CogniFit
- Peak
- Fit Brains

Concept two: Priming
Preparing is an idea where certain words, pictures, or articles can influence our cerebrum. This affects how you decide.

For instance, when you consider espresso, the top brand or organization, most of us think it is Starbucks. That is because our way of life and society has "prepared us" to do as such. Wherever we look, we see logos and advertisements for Starbucks. We see individuals on TV drinking Starbucks while strolling through New York City. This is preparing us to make a relationship to espresso when we see or hear certain words.

Suppose you need to put resources into an espresso organization. Utilizing the model above, you may consider Starbucks the best investment. Yet, this could be because of the preparation you've encountered. You may think Starbucks is the best investment since everybody drinks it. You may likewise connect Starbucks with New York and New York with abundance. This may make you look past a more modest espresso organization that is a superior investment.

Preparing is a typical result of the way of life we live in. It pushes us to settle on investment decisions we may think nothing about. It happens constantly, yet we do it without knowing.

Examination of the organization and its industry top to bottom before contributing. Moderate down and think (utilize your framework two) preceding heading out to get one of the "10 Hottest Stocks for Christmas." You may be getting prepared.

Here are two of the best assets for finding out about an organization:

- EDGAR Database: the financial information for any traded on an open market organization
- Yahoo! Finance and Yahoo! Account Markets: both incredible assets for getting familiar with your organization, its rivals, and the market it is in

Concept three: Snap decisions and misrepresentation

Two fundamental ideas can influence how you pick investments. The first is the corona impact. This is your brain's languid propensity to relate two irrelevant things. It tends to be an individual, item, or circumstance and is generally a consequence of a past idea or information point you have.

For instance: You own an iPhone, MacBook, and iPad. You're an Apple enthusiast, and you love their items. Along these lines (and this lone), you believe that Apple would make the best vehicles. However, because they make fantastic hardware doesn't mean they would make superb vehicles.

The subsequent idea is the affirmation inclination. This one is difficult and happens regularly. It's the propensity for us to concur with opinions and conclusions that are following our convictions.

For example, suppose that you feel that Miller Lite is a decent brew. Suppose I am a renowned brewmaster. If I revealed to you that Miller Lite was the best brew, however, it was likewise helpful for you, you would concur with me. Without a doubt, you'd currently feel that Miller Lite was the best lager, not simply a decent brew. I, the master, presently affirmed your assessment.

Kow your organization all around; at that point, structure your assessment. Utilize the assets from idea two as a benchmark. At that point, make it a stride further by taking a gander at the other top to bottom examination. See things like a stock's danger rating, verifiable information and patterns, and investigator's examination reports.

Here are three all-around regarded premium stock exploration locales for you to investigate:

- Morningstar
- Zacks Premium

- S&P Capital IQ

Toward the day's end, you need to choose how significant contributions is to you. It is safe to say that you are OK with making sluggish, imprudent choices? Or on the other hand, would you rather invest a little Momentum and exertion to settle on a more good choice?

Regardless of whether you're putting resources into Zhu Pets or stocks and bonds, understanding these ideas (and applying methods to make your cerebrum work for you) will make you a superior financial backer over the long haul.

Warren Buffet: The Ultimate Value Investor

In any case, in the event that you are a genuine worth financial backer, you needn't bother with anybody to persuade you to have to remain in it for the since quite a while ago run since this strategy is planned around the possibility that one should purchase organizations—not stocks. That implies the financial backer should think about the 10,000 foot view, not an impermanent knockout execution. Individuals regularly refer to unbelievable financial backer Warren Buffet as the encapsulation of a worth financial backer. He gets his work done—some of the time for quite a long time. Yet, when he's prepared, he bets everything and is submitted as long as possible.

Consider Buffett's words when he made a significant investment in the carrier business. He clarified that aircrafts "had an awful first century." Then he said, "And they moved a terrible century, I hope."2 This reasoning embodies a significant part of the worth contributing methodology. Decisions depend on many years of patterns and in light of many years of future execution.

For the individuals who don't have the opportunity to perform comprehensive examination, the value income proportion (P/E) has become the essential instrument for rapidly recognizing underestimated or modest stocks. This is a solitary number that comes from isolating a stock's offer cost by its profit per share (EPS). A lower P/E proportion implies you're paying less per $1 of current profit. Worth financial backers look for organizations with a low P/E proportion.

While utilizing the P/E proportion is a decent beginning, a few specialists caution this estimation alone isn't sufficient to make the strategy work. Exploration distributed in the Financial Analysts Journal confirmed that "Quantitative investment procedures dependent on such proportions are bad substitutes for esteem contributing methodologies that utilization an exhaustive methodology in recognizing undervalued protections." The explanation, as per their work, is that financial backers are frequently tricked by low P/E proportion stocks dependent on incidentally expanded bookkeeping numbers. These low figures are, in numerous occasions, the aftereffect of a dishonestly high income figure (the denominator). At the point when genuine income are accounted for (not simply guage) they're frequently lower. This outcomes in a "inversion to the mean." The P/E proportion goes up and the worth the financial backer sought after is gone.

On the off chance that utilizing the P/E proportion alone is defective, how should a financial backer deal with discover genuine worth stocks? The analysts recommend, "Quantitative ways to deal with distinguishing these twists—like joining predictable worth with Momentum, quality and productivity measures—can help in keeping away from these 'esteem traps.'"

In this day and age, we need everything improved.

The PC age has made us so subject to innovation. In a manner, it's acceptable because we would now be able to zero in on our work and let our devices do the challenging work. The accompanying rundown is sites to help you research quicker and deal with your money better.

That way, you can put your consideration on the principal thing;

- time
- loved ones
- building riches

Alert: don't burn through a lot of time going through each site. It's ideal to utilize the locales that will profit your style of exploration. NOT to sit around messing with everything. It's so natural to turn upward and understand an hour has passed and everything you've done is surf the web.

So right away, here are the best contributing and money instruments to assist you with completing things quicker.

Earnings Cast

Veteran financial backers realize that tuning in to income call can give critical contributing understanding. You can distinguish whether the supervisory group is over hopeful, regardless of whether they are straight talkers or more like sales reps.

Trefis

This site fundamentally assists clients with dissecting the income streams for the organizations that are covered. Rather than simply seeing a solitary number that addresses income, you can perceive how it is separated.

Likewise, you can change the development of income sections to think of new valuations for what the stock would be worth.

Estimize

Estimize is the place where you can look at what individuals are expecting the EPS gauge to be. It's generally for subsequent quarter profit; however, the area of the site is to show how better standard people can assess EPS over investigators.

Street of Walls

This site is for individuals searching for work in Wallstreet. However, their preparation area is magnificent for instruction.

The site gives preparing to help you become top ability paying little heed to your experience.

Before you plunge into the meat of the substance, if you haven't joined with your email for our free investment assets, do as such.

I'll quickly send you additional stock proportions notes, agendas, accounting pages and other downloads you can prevail with.

Mint

Mint is extraordinary to keep an idea about your accounting records. Contributing is magnificent, and yet, it's likewise essential to hold your budgets within proper limits.

With XBRL, numerous organizations are coming out with approaches to make SEC filings and search simpler and better.

The solitary blow is that the US House of Representatives has passed a bill where organizations making under $250m in income are not needed to record utilizing XBRL.

Rank and Filed

It very well may be exceptionally overwhelming and tedious with regards to perusing the SEC records. Rank and Filed is a great site to make perusing Sec filings simpler.

This is what Rank and Filed are in their own words:

It resembles the SEC's EDGAR data set, yet for people.

BamSEC

This is a charge based assistance yet must be incorporated because it's clean thus simple to utilize. Enter a ticker into their pursuit bar, and you'll get a rundown of the relative multitude of filings in a simple to peruse and look through design.

Finviz

Heaps of market information and perceptions. Far superior to the more significant part of the other more excellent account destinations.

You can peruse all accessible stock information. There are channels, signals and stock screens you can use to filter through all the data.

Morningstar

Excellent site for stock examination, five years of free financial information and basics.

The articles are superior to most locales, yet they centre around generally huge covers.

gurufocus

GuruFocus.com is a quality worth contributing site offering heaps of information and investigation and spot an extraordinary accentuation on what the "master" financial backers are doing and holding.

Top Asset Management Tools
The pattern in money these days is mechanized portfolio the executives. For individuals who need an uninvolved technique for contributing, this is presumably the ideal approach to minor expenses.

SigFig

They rebranded their site. It used to be a pink pig all over the place; however, they've exchanged their plan of action to be more centred around auto portfolio the executives.

Money never dozes, and neither do we. Our unprejudiced calculations are continually observing your investments, giving a fair portfolio customized only for you.

You can likewise connect up your money market funds to follow execution and other details.

Personal Capital

One of the new and hot resources the board devices available. You don't need to pursue any paid administrations, yet you'll get calls once in a while to join their portfolio of the executive's administration.

Yet, if you contribute all alone, utilizing their portfolio apparatus isn't so awful.

At the point when you become an investment customer, we'll match you with a group of guides who will become acquainted with you, your novel financial circumstance, and your objectives.

Advancement

Same as the other two; however, I trust Betterment has been around longer.

Another decision to handily deal with your portfolio and put it on autopilot.

Put resources into a broadened arrangement of stock and bond ETFs intended for ideal anticipated returns.

You will set aside time and cash since everything is robotized with a low administration charge.

Bloomberg Visual Data

From MLB groups esteem, the 2014 World Cup, and tycoons record, Bloomberg visual information gives you a graphic portrayal of data making it drawing in and more apparent.

It's as yet youthful, yet the substance is vibrant, and you can undoubtedly comprehend the information, which would be inconceivable if it was recorded on a table.

XBRL

A representation apparatus from the XBRL consortium to show which organizations and enterprises have recorded with the SEC.

XBRL has been moving for quite a while and is developing; in any case, it endured a new shot when the House of Representatives declared that organizations with under $250m in income don't need to record utilizing XBRL.

That is 60% of all open organizations. We'll perceive how XBRL defeats this. Up to that point, it is anything but innovation to depend 100% on.

TradingView

This simple to-utilize diagramming site will give you continuous data and necessary market experiences—incredible programming for diagrams.

The best on the web stock graphs and a local area of financial backers who are energetic about sharing exchanging thoughts.

With only a single tick, you can see live graphs and explained articles put together by local area individuals.

StockCharts

It still has a burdensome mid-2000 UI, yet it works and is quite possibly the most famous destination for outlines if you're into the specialized examination.

Who figured making top-notch financial outlines could be so natural? We have the apparatuses, instructive data, well-qualified suppositions, and backing you need to comprehend the business sectors. Recall that while anybody can utilize our free instruments, just endorsers approach our most impressive highlights.

What's the Message?

The message here is that worth contributing can work insofar as the financial backer is in it as long as possible and is set up to apply some genuine exertion and examination to their stock determination. Those willing to place the work in and stay remain to acquire. One investigation from Dodge and Cox discovered that esteem procedures almost consistently beat development methodologies "over skylines of 10 years or more." The examination proceeds to clarify that esteem systems have failed to meet expectations development techniques for a 10-year time span in only three periods in the course of the most recent 90 years. Those periods were the Great Depression (1929-1939/40), the Technology Stock Bubble (1989-1999), and the period 2004-2014/15.

Strategy 2: Growth Investing

Maybe then search for ease bargains; financial development backers need investments that offer solid potential gain potential regarding the future income of stocks. It very well may be said that a development financial backer is regularly searching for the "following huge thing." Growth contributing, nonetheless, is anything but a foolish hug of theoretical contributing. Maybe, it includes assessing a stock's present wellbeing just as its capability to develop.

A development financial backer considers the possibilities of the business wherein the stock flourishes. You may ask, for instance, if there's a future for electric vehicles before putting resources into Tesla. Or then again, you may contemplate whether A.I. will turn into an installation of ordinary living before putting resources into an innovation organization. There should be proof of an endless and hearty hunger for the organization's administrations or items if it will develop. Financial backers can address this inquiry by taking a gander at an organization's new history. Basically: A development stock ought to be growing. The organization ought to have a reliable pattern of solid profit and income, meaning an ability to follow through on development assumptions.

A downside to development contributing is an absence of profits. On the off chance that an organization is in development mode, it frequently needs funding to support its extension. This doesn't leave a lot (or any) cash left for profit installments. In addition, with quicker profit development comes higher valuations which are, for most financial backers, a higher danger recommendation.

Does Growth Investing Work?

As the examination above demonstrates, esteem contributing will, in general, beat development contributing over the long haul. These discoveries don't mean a development financial backer can't benefit from the strategy; it simply implies a development strategy doesn't usually create the degree of profits seen with esteem contributing. However, as per an investigation from New York University's Stern School of Business, "While development contributing fails to meet expectations esteem contributing, particularly throughout long time-frames, it is additionally evident that there are sub-periods, where development contributing dominates." The test is deciding when these "sub-periods" will happen.

Strangely, deciding the periods when a development strategy is ready to perform may mean taking a gander at the total national output (GDP). Take the time somewhere in the range of 2000 and 2015, when a development strategy beat a worth plan in seven years. During five of these years, the GDP development rate was underneath 2%. Then, a worth approach won in nine years, and in seven of those years, the GDP was above 2%. Consequently, it makes sense that a development strategy might be more effective during times of diminishing GDP.

Some development contributing style doubters caution that "development at any cost" is a risky methodology. Such a drive brought about the tech bubble, which disintegrated a large number of portfolios. "Absurd decade, the normal development stock has returned 159% versus only 89% for esteem," as indicated by Money magazine's Investor's Guide 2018.

Stock market contributing isn't close to as messy as many Wall Street experts would have you accept. Actually, by applying a reliable methodology that praises a couple of key financial standards - like broadening, judiciousness, and long haul thinking - anybody can assemble a portfolio custom-made to their specific retirement objectives.

Development contributing is perhaps the most mainstream styles out there, and here we'll investigate the means associated with exploiting this strategy.

What is growth investing?

To start with, it's useful to comprehend what development contributing is - and what it isn't. The methodology alludes to purchasing stocks connected to organizations that have alluring qualities their opponents need. These can incorporate effectively quantifiable things, for example, market-beating development rates in deals or potentially profit. Likewise, they can contain more subjective factors like solid client unwavering ness, a significant brand, or many deep canals.

Development stocks will, in general, stand firm on good footings in arising industry specialities that component long runways for extension in front of them. Because of this alluring potential and the strangely solid achievement, the business has had. Lately, a development stock is evaluated at a top-notch that mirrors the idealism financial backers have in the organization. Thus, the least difficult approach to realize whether you're taking a gander at a development stock is if its valuation, generally its cost to-profit numerous, is high compared with the more extensive market and its industry peers.

This methodology appears differently about esteem contributing, which centres around stocks that have become undesirable on Wall

Street. These are stocks with lower valuations that reflect more unassuming deals and benefit possibilities. Both investment procedures can work whenever applied reliably. However, financial backers, for the most part, incline toward one side of the range or the other.

So since you realize development contributing is for you, we should investigate the means engaged with completely benefiting from the strategy.

Step 1: Prepare your finances.

A decent dependable guideline is that you shouldn't accept stocks with the cash you get you'll require in the following five years at any rate. That is because while the market, for the most part, ascends over the long haul, it as often as possible posts sharp drops of 10%, 20%, or more that happen abruptly. Probably the greatest mix-up you can make as a financial backer is setting yourself in a place to be compelled to sell stocks during one of these down periods. In a perfect world, you'll rather be prepared to purchase supplies when most others are selling.

Step 2: Get comfortable with growth approaches.

Presently that you're on the way toward more grounded funds, it's an ideal opportunity to arm yourself with another useful asset: information. There are a couple of kinds of development contributing techniques you can decide to follow.

For instance, you can zero in just on huge, grounded organizations that, as of now, have a background marked by producing positive income. Your methodology could be moored in quantitative measurements that fit in stock screeners, like working edge, return on contributed capital and yearly compound development. Then again, numerous development financial backers mean to buy the best-performing organizations around, as proven by their steady market share gains, with to lesser degree attention on share costs.

It regularly bodes well to centre your buys in enterprises and organizations you know especially well. Regardless of whether that is because you have insight in, say, the eatery business or in working for a cloud programming administrations business, that information will assist you with assessing investments as potential purchase up-and-comers. It's generally desirable to know a ton about a little fragment of organizations than to see slightly about a wide scope of organizations.

However, what is basic to your profits is that you reliably apply the strategy you pick and stay away from the compulsion to hop, starting with one methodology then onto the next, basically because all accounts work better right now. That technique is classified as "pursuing returns," and it's a certain method to fail to meet expectations of the market over the long haul.

Keep away from that destiny by getting comfortable with the fundamentals of this stock market contributing strategy. Perusing a couple of moral development donating books is an incredible spot to begin, and afterwards, familiarize yourself with the bosses in the field.

For instance, T. Rowe Price is credited similar to the dad of development contributing, and, even though he resigned from the field in 1971, his impact is as yet being felt today. Cost advocated the possibility that an organization's profit development could be projected out over numerous years, which moved financial backers' intuition when stocks were viewed as repeating, momentary investments.

Warren Buffett is typically portrayed as a worth financial backer, yet components of his methodology are of the development assortment. This statement from Buffett is an exemplary enunciation of the strategy: "It's far superior to purchase an awesome organization at a reasonable cost than a reasonable organization at a brilliant cost." all in all, the cost is a significant piece of any investment; however the strength of the business ostensibly matters similarly to such an extent, if not more.

Step 3: Stock selection

Presently it's an ideal opportunity to plan to start making investments. This piece of the interaction begins with choosing exactly how much money you need to designate toward your development investment strategy. If you're shiny new to the methodology, it may bode well to begin a little with, say, 10% of your portfolio reserves. As you get more familiar with the instability and develop experience contributing through various sorts of markets (rallies, droops, and everything in the middle), this proportion can rise.

Hazard assumes a major part in this decision, as well, since development stocks are viewed as more Momentumful, and subsequently, more unstable than guarded stocks. That is why a more extended time skyline by and large permits greater adaptability to lean your portfolio toward this contributing style.

A decent method to check whether you have excessively high distribution toward development stocks is if your portfolio makes you restless. On the off chance that you wind up stressed over likely misfortunes or worrying over past market drops, you should lessen your openness to singular development stocks for more various choices.

Buying growth funds

The simplest method to acquire openness to a different scope of development stocks is through an asset. Numerous retirement plans highlight development centred choices, and these could shape the premise of your contributing strategy.

Venturing farther into self-coordinated decisions, consider buying a development based list store. File reserves are ideal investment vehicles since they convey broadening at lower costs than with shared assets. In contrast to common assets controlled by investment administrators who attempt to beat the market, file finances use PC calculations to match the arrival of the business benchmark. Since most investment chiefs miss the mark concerning that benchmark, you'll typically wind up on top of things with a file store.

Index Fund	Annual Expense	Turnover
Vanguard Growth Index Fund	0.17%	6%
SPDR S&P 500 Growth ETF	0.04%	20%
iShares Russell 1000 Growth ETF	0.2%	13%

Screening for growth stocks

If you'd prefer to move into the DIY domain, you can purchase singular development stocks. This methodology has the highest potential for market-beating returns, yet it likewise conveys considerably more danger than putting resources into a differentiated asset.

To discover development stocks, screen for elements, for example, these:

- Better than expected development in income per share or the benefits the organization produces every year.
- Better than expected benefit (working edge or gross edge), or the level of deals an organization transforms into services.
- High authentic development in income or deals.
- The exceptional yield on contributed capital is a proportion of how effectively an organization goes through its money.

Simultaneously, you'll need to keep an eye out for warnings that raise the hazard of a business. A couple of models:

- The organization booked a yearly total deficit in the previous three years. This isn't a major issue for most development financial backers, yet it recommends an organization presently can't seem to fabricate a manageable plan of action.
- The organization conveys a low market capitalization (of, for instance, underneath $500 million). Small stocks are powerless against greater contenders and numerous different interruptions that could undermine their whole organizations. Thus, countless financial backers feel good starting their inquiry in the "mid-cap" scope of stocks.
- There was a new administration purge, especially in the CEO position.
- Deals or potentially productivity is falling. It will not qualify as a development stock if its centre working measurements are going lower.

Step 4: Maximize returns.

Development stocks will, in general, be unpredictable, and keeping in mind that your point ought to be to hold every investment for at least quite a while, you'll, in any case, need to watch out for critical estimating changes for a couple of key reasons.

On the off chance that a segment of your property has acquired such an excess of significant worth that it overwhelms your portfolio, it may bode well to diminish your openness by rebalancing your portfolio.

On the off chance that a stock transcends your gauge of its worth, you can think about selling it, particularly if you've recognized other, all the more sensibly valued investments to coordinate the assets toward.

If the organization has hit a tough situation that has broken your unique investment theory or explained you purchased the stock in any case, you should sell. A wrecked postulation may incorporate significant stumbles by the supervisory crew, a drawn-out decrease in estimating Momentum, or disturbance by a lower-evaluated contender.

These are only a portion of the numerous reasons a financial backer should make changes by their portfolio by choosing to sell a stock.

Accepting you got your work done when you at first bought your stocks, as a rule, your work will add up to standing by, being patient, and permitting the Momentum of intensifying re-visitations of development to its full effect on your portfolio throughout the following 10, 20, or 30 years and that's just the beginning.

Investing in Hot Sectors

One methodology development financial backers can take is to put resources into stocks, common assets, and ETFs dependent on explicit areas and businesses. The achievement of organizations in different regions changes over the long haul. Notwithstanding, it's typically genuinely simple to recognize areas that are "hot" in the feeling of creating better than expected returns for traded on an open market organization.

For instance, two areas that have been especially hot for years and years are medical services and innovation. Organizations that manage innovation, mechanical advances, or are continually putting out new equipment, programming, and gadgets are good picks for financial development backers. The equivalent is valid for organizations in the medical care area. Consider it consistently: Everyone, sooner or later, necessities to focus on their wellbeing, and some organizations are continually growing new prescriptions, treatments, medicines, and places to go to get to this consideration. The medical care area will probably keep getting a charge out of fast development as it serves a maturing child of post-war America age. Indeed, these two areas are connected, as numerous new mechanical improvements have been propelling in medical services innovation.

Development financial backers can work on area contributing by exploiting investment vehicles, such as common assets and ETFs containing a bin of stocks connected to explicit regions. ETFs are an inexorably mainstream investment alternative because of their overall liquidity and lower exchange costs compared to shared assets.

Understanding Earnings

For financial development backers in stocks, understanding an organization's net income is fundamental. This doesn't mean knowing their present income, yet considering their verifiable profit also since this empowers a financial backer to assess current yield comparative with an organization's previous exhibition. Additionally, investigating an organization's income history gives a clearer sign of the organization's likelihood of producing higher future profit.

A high-profit execution in a given quarter or year may address a one-time oddity in an organization's presentation, a proceeding with the pattern, or a specific point in an income cycle that the organization keeps rehashing after some time.

It's additionally imperative to comprehend that even organizations with moderately low, or in some cases even worse, income may, in any case, be a decent pick for a development financial backer. Recollect that profit are what's leftover in the wake of taking away all creation, marketing, working, work, and expense costs from an organization's gross income. On numerous occasions, more modest organizations endeavour to make a forward leap by piping more capital toward developing their business, which may contrarily affect their income in the short run, however over the long haul, creating more significant yields more important benefits for financial backers. In such a circumstance, shrewd financial backers think about different variables, like the nature of an organization's administration, to discover hints concerning the organization's actual development potential.

Growth Investing Through Value Investing

Development financial backers are adequately esteemed financial backers once in a while, in that they search out organizations whose stock might be presently underestimated because of reasons that might be pretty much as straightforward as the way that the organization is moderately new and has not yet grabbed the eye of numerous investment experts or asset directors.

The objective is to get up shares at a low cost of an organization that is very much situated to appreciate a sizeable and proceeded with the flood in development. There are various potential approaches to distinguishing such organizations, one of which we've effectively addressed – taking a gander at organizations in hot areas. Financial backers who can determine another very much oversaw and all around supported organization essential for a desirable location can frequently receive significant benefits. Another conceivable methodology is to inspect organizations on the downslope; for example, those who have gone through insolvency or redesign will probably endure and recuperate.

Using the Price-to-Earnings Ratio

The value/profit (P/E) proportion is an apparatus that financial development backers regularly use to help them pick stocks to put resources into. As the proportion's name makes apparent, you need to comprehend an organization's profit before you can adequately utilize the instrument.

As a rule, the higher the P/E proportion, the more prominent the danger financial backers will take on an organization due to its projected income and development rate.

The P/E proportion is especially valuable for financial development backers attempting to look at organizations that work in a similar industry. In set up businesses and areas, there will, in general, be normal P/E proportions for that specific industry or size. Knowing such industry or area midpoints makes an organization's P/E balance a considerably more helpful number than essentially viewing it in contrast with the market in general.

Taking a gander at an organization's P/E proportion stays a valuable logical device for financial development backers; however, adding thought of another key economic measurement can assist with fining tune your investment picks.

Using the Price-to-Book Ratio

The cost to-book proportion – or P/B proportion – is frequently viewed as more the essential scientific measurement of significant worth financial backers than financial development backers. Nonetheless, the truth of the matter is that the P/B proportion can likewise be used as a powerful apparatus in recognizing stocks with high development potential.

The P/B proportion is determined by separating a stock's for every offer cost by the book esteem per share. To decide the book worth of stock, the favoured stock that has been given should be deducted from the all-out stockholder value. All introductory offers should then partition the figure determined from this takeaway as yet exceptional. The last number is the organization's book esteem per portion of the stock. It is frequently useful for financial backers, particularly development financial backers, to contrast an organization's book esteem with its market esteem. This examination can give a decent sign of whether a stock is underestimated or exaggerated. Organizations with high development potential are habitually underestimated because of heftier obligation burdens and capital consumptions.

How about we put this proportion to utilize. For this model, we will use the S&P 500 Index. A development financial backer would, in principle, investigate the entirety of the stocks, computing or looking into the P/B proportion for each. Notwithstanding how the stores are recorded, the development financial backer could improve them as indicated by their P/B ratio, beginning with the most important numbers and finishing with the least. The organizations that fall inside the top third of the rundown would be viewed as possibly great development stock picks. Remember that this is certainly not an exact science yet, to a greater extent, an accommodating model that financial development backers can utilize to distinguish and add stocks with the best potential for development to their portfolios.

High-Risk Growth Investments

Development putting may likewise reach out into investments past customary stock market contributing.

Putting resources into high-hazard development investments – likewise alluded to as speculative investments – is a methodology that isn't appropriate for financial backers with a low edge for hazard. This strategy is most suitable for economic development backers searching for the greatest benefits inside a generally brief timeframe casing and who have adequate investment money to support them during potential times of misfortunes.

High-hazard investments incorporate such things as fates, alternatives contracts, foreign cash trade (forex), penny stocks, and theoretical land, for example, land that hasn't been created. These investments imply more danger in that they offer no ensured return. Their worth will, in general, change rapidly (at the end of the day, they're dependent upon more noteworthy unpredictability). In any case, the draw for some financial backers is that when such investments pay off, they frequently pay off huge.

In case you're thinking about any of these investments, recollect that exploration is critical to progress. More so than the normal stock or bond financial backer, you need to realize the market you're putting resources into well indeed. Since progress depends greatly on theory, we unequivocally suggest that lone experienced financial backers roll the dice on investment resources, for example, these.

Popular Types of Growth Investments

A couple of fundamental classifications of resources have verifiably shown the best development potential. Every one of them includes the value in some structure, and they generally accompany a more significant level of hazard. Individuals have a wide range of styles and tastes regarding money, yet bringing in your money development is normally viewed as the most basic investment objective. The ideal approach to achieve this objective will differ as per factors like the financial backer's danger resilience and time skyline. In any case, there are some key standards and procedures that are material to a wide range of kinds of financial backers and development systems.

Kinds of development investments incorporate the accompanying:

Small-Cap Stocks

The size of an organization depends on its market capitalization or total assets. There is no careful, widespread meaning of what is viewed as a "little cap" contrasted with miniature, mid or huge cap. Yet, most examiners characterize any organization with a capitalization of between $300 million and $2 billion as a little cap firm.

Organizations in this classification are generally still in their underlying period of development, and their stocks have the potential for generous appreciation in cost. Little cap stocks usually have posted more significant yields than their blue-chip cousins, yet they are likewise impressively more unstable and convey a more serious level of hazard. Little cap stocks have additionally frequently beaten enormous cap stocks during times of recovery from downturns.

Technology and Healthcare Stocks

Organizations that grow new advances or offer developments in medical services can be magnificent decisions for financial backers searching for a grand slam play in their portfolios. The stocks of organizations that create famous or progressive items can rise dramatically in cost in a generally brief timeframe.

For instance, the cost of Pfizer (PFE) was just shy of $5 an offer in 1994 preceding Viagra was delivered. This blockbuster drug took the organization's stock cost to above $30 a bid over the following five years on the FDA endorsement of the medication in 1998. Now and again, a development stock can go on a wild ride. Streaming media organization (ROKU) flooded in the months after its first sale of stock (IPO) in the fall of 2017 to withdraw towards the end cost from its first day of exchanging only a couple of short months after the fact.

Speculative Investments

Daredevils and theorists look to high-chance development instruments, for example, penny stocks, fates and alternatives contracts, unfamiliar cash and theoretical land like lacking area. There are additionally oil and gas boring organizations and private value for Momentumful financial backers in big league salary sections. The individuals who pick the correct decisions in this field can see a profit from the capital of commonly their underlying investment; however, they can likewise frequently lose each penny of their head.

Researching Growth Stocks

There are a few key factors that should be viewed while assessing investment development. The pace of development, the sum and kind of hazard and different components of putting assume a great part in the measure of money that financial backers leave with.

With regards to stocks, a portion of the information that financial development backers and experts analyze incorporate the accompanying:

Return on Equity (ROE)

ROE is a numerical articulation of how productively a partnership can make a benefit. It is measured as a rate that addresses the organization's overall gain (which implies the pay staying after the favoured stockholders have been paid, however, before the regular stock profits are paid) separated by the absolute value of the investors.

For instance, if one organization has all out investor value of $100 million while another organization has an investment value of $300 million and the two organizations have total compensation for the time of $75 million, at that point, the organization with the more modest investor value is giving a more prominent profit from value since it is procuring a similar overall gain with less weight.

Increasing Earnings Per Share (EPS)

Even though a few kinds of EPS and the measure of money acquired on a for each offer premise doesn't recount the entire tale about how a business is run, an organization whose income for every offer is expanding over the long run is presumably accomplishing something right. Financial backers regularly look for organizations with an expanding EPS, yet further examination ought to be done to guarantee that the EPS numbers are the consequence of certifiable income from real transactions.

Projected Earnings

Numerous informal investors and momentary financial backers give close consideration to projected income declarations since they can have both prompt and future impacts on an organization's stock cost. Indeed, numerous financial backers bring in money exchanging income declarations.

For instance, when an organization's projected profit come in higher than anticipated, the stock cost will regularly rise rapidly and afterwards pattern down before very long. However, reliable positive projected income reports will assist the stock with ascending over the long run.

Development Investing Variables

While there is no conclusive rundown of complex measurements to manage a development strategy, a couple of elements financial backer ought to consider. An examination from Merrill Lynch, for instance, discovered that development stocks beat during times of falling loan costs. It's essential to remember that development stocks are frequently quick to get hit whenever there's any hint of a slump in the economy.

Development financial backers likewise need to painstakingly consider the administration ability of a business' leader group. Accomplishing development is among the most troublesome difficulties for a firm. In this way, a heavenly administration group is required. Financial backers should observe how the group performs and the methods by which it accomplishes development. Development is of little worth if it's completed with substantial getting. Simultaneously, financial backers ought to assess the opposition. An organization may appreciate a heavenly story, yet on the off chance that its essential item is handily reproduced, the drawn-out possibilities are faint.

GoPro is a perfect representation of this marvel. The once high-flying stock has seen regular yearly income decays since 2015. "Soon after its introduction, shares dramatically multiplied the IPO cost of $24 to as much as $87," the Wall Street Journal reported. The stock has exchanged well underneath its IPO cost. Quite a bit of this end is ascribed to the effortlessly imitated plan. GoPro is, at its centre, a little camera in a container. The rising notoriety and nature of cell phone cameras offer a modest option in contrast to paying $400 to $600 for a one-work piece of gear. In addition, the organization has been fruitless at planning and delivering new items, which is an essential advance to supporting development—something development financial backers should consider.

Makes a good growth stock
To change development putting into a manageable strategy, financial backers should figure out how to distinguish values that have the most potential to become development stocks. While the accompanying rundown isn't thorough, here are the three significant standards for spotting great development stocks:

Search for new, high-rising enterprises: The principal activity is to search for more up to date ventures and areas displaying more grounded than normal development.

"Development putting tends to live in more current enterprises where client acknowledgment is developing from an exceptionally low level, say cell phones as a chronicled model. Development stocks are distinguished by how quick their incomes and profit are developing comparative with the market," says Massocca.

It's insufficient for financial backers to distinguish development areas and put resources into any beginning phase organization they can discover. It's also imperative to get your work done on what any given organization is doing and how they fit into their industry.

Assess future income power: Another significant territory to consider is the future income Momentum of an organization, which means its capacity to produce benefits over the long haul. This should be possible by looking at its profit from resources (ROA) and its profit from value (ROE), just like its present incomes, resources, and benefits.

"While choosing development stocks, it is imperative to comprehend the plan of action of the organizationorganization, their profit power into the future," says Niladri Mukherjee.

Evaluate the nature of senior administration: obviously, it's insufficient to just gander at an organization's area and its present-day financials. If you need a smart thought of whether it truly can develop soundly into the future, you'll likewise have to think about the nature of its senior administration.

This implies seeing its board and leaders, checking their experience and history. If nobody in senior administration has any significant level of involvement, it could be unsafe to expect that the organization will perform unequivocally and reasonably.

Besides scouring new companies and developing markets, one enticement might be recognizing potential development stocks by searching for starting public contributions. Such IPOs will, in general, be held by organizations in high-development areas and may guarantee higher-than-normal returns.

Notwithstanding, research proposes that IPOs aren't just about as beneficial as many may expect, with authentic information gathered by the University of Florida's Jay Ritter showing that around 60% of IPOs have negative returns for a very long time following their openings.

Notwithstanding such risks, one more secure choice might be to put resources into a common asset or ETF, which tracks development stocks and areas, holding an assortment of organizations in its portfolio.

"An ETF gives a financially savvy approach to get openness to a list of development stocks," says Niladri Mukherjee.

Probably the most well-known development ETFs include:

- iShares Russell 1000 Growth ETF
- Invesco QQQ ETF
- Vanguard Information Technology ETF
- O'Shares Global Internet Giants ETF

For instance, the iShares Russell 1000 Growth ETF tracks around 500 of the best-performing enormous U.S. stocks. It recorded an arrival of 37.2% for the year to September 2020, contrasted with an appearance of 13% and 6.6%, separately, for the S&P 500 and the Dow Jones. The NASDAQ rose by 45.8% over a similar period, so not all high-development assets might be more productive than only putting resources into an investment that tracks a file.

In like manner, here's a little choice of the most prominent and best-performing development shared assets:

- Fidelity Trend Fund
- Zevenbergen Growth Fund
- T. Rowe Price Blue Chip Growth Fund
- Franklin DynaTech Fund

Chapter 2: Momentum Investing

Momentum financial backers ride the wave. They accept victors continue winning, and washouts continue to lose. They hope to purchase stocks encountering an upturn. Since they take failures to keep on dropping, they may decide to short-sell those protections. In any case, short-selling is an unsafe practice. More on that later.

Consider Momentum financial backers specialized investigators. This implies they utilize a rigorously information-driven way to deal with exchanging and search at designs in stock costs to manage their buying choices. Momentum financial backers act in insubordination of the productive market speculation (EMH). This speculation expresses that resource costs completely mirror all data accessible to the general population. It's hard to accept this assertion and be a Momentum financial backer, given that the strategy looks to profit by underestimated and exaggerated values.

The Father of Momentum Investing

Even though not the primary Momentum financial backer, Richard Driehaus took the training and made it into the strategy he used to run his assets. His way of thinking was that more money could be caused by "purchasing high and selling higher" than purchasing undervalued stocks and hanging tight for the market to rethink them.

Driehaus trusted in selling the washouts and allowing the champs to ride while re-putting the money from the failures in different stocks that were starting to bubble. Large numbers of the procedures he utilized turned into the rudiments of what is currently called Momentum contributing.

Precepts of Momentum Investing

Momentum contributing looks to exploit market unpredictability by taking momentary situations in which stocks are going up and selling them when they indicate going down. The financial backer, at that point, moves the cash flow to new positions. For this situation, the market unpredictability resembles waves in the sea. A Momentum financial backer cruises up the peak of one to leap to the next wave before the primary wave crashes down once more.

A Momentum financial backer hopes to exploit financial backer crowding by standing out and being the first to take the money and run.

Elements of Momentum Investing

Exchanging Momentum markets require modern danger the board rules to address unpredictability, packing, and covered up traps that decrease benefits. Market players regularly disregard these principles; dazed by a mind-boggling dread, they'll miss the assembly or selloff while every other person books bonus benefits. The standards can be separated into five components:

- Determination, or what values you pick
- Hazard rotate around timing in opening and shutting the exchanges
- Section timing implies getting into the business early
- Position the board couples wide spreads and your holding period
- Leave focuses on requiring reliable graphing

Momentum Security Selection

Pick fluid protections while taking part in Momentum techniques. Avoid utilized or reverse ETFs because their value swings don't precisely follow basic records or fates markets because of complex asset development. Standard subsidizes make magnificent exchanging vehicles; however, they will generally crush through more modest rate gains and misfortunes contrasted and singular protections.

Search out protections that exchange over 5 million offers each day at whatever point conceivable. Numerous well-known stocks meet these rules. However, even common buoy issues can transform into exceptionally fluid instruments when news stream and extreme passionate responses attract market players from different sources.

Save watch for "today's special," when new items, divisions or ideas catch the public's creative mind, driving experts to discard computations and re-process benefit gauges. Biotechs and little to medium size innovation organizations make a liberal inventory of these story stocks.

Tight Risk Control

The dangerous side of the condition should be tended to in detail, or the Momentum strategy will come up short. The traps of Momentum exchanging include:

- I was hopping into a position too early before an Momentum move is affirmed.
- They are shutting the position past the point of no return after immersion has been reached.
- You neglect to keep your eyes on the screen, missing evolving patterns, inversions or indications of information that shock the market.

- They are keeping a position open for the time being. Stocks are especially defenceless to outside factors happening after the end of that day's exchanging – these components could cause fundamentally various costs and examples the following day.
- You neglect to act rapidly to close a terrible position, consequently riding the Momentum train the incorrect path down the tracks.

Perfect Entry Timing

The best Momentum exchanges come when a news stun hits, setting off rapid development starting with one value level then onto the next. Thus, this sets off purchasing or selling signals for discerning players who hop in and are remunerated with moment benefits. Another group of Momentum capital enters as the exchange develops, producing counter swings that shake out powerless hands. The hot money populace at long last hits a limit, setting off unpredictable whipsaws and significant inversions.

Early positions offer the best price with the least danger while maturing patterns should be kept away from no matter what. The inverse occurs in real situations because most merchants don't see the chance until late in the cycle and afterwards neglect to act until every other person hops in.

Position Management

The board set aside some effort to dominate because these protections frequently convey wide bid/ask spreads. Wide spreads require bigger development in support of yourself to arrive at productivity while likewise crushing through wide intraday ranges that uncover stops—even though technicals stay flawless.

Pick your holding period astutely because hazard expands the more you stay situated. Day exchanging functions admirably with Momentum techniques; however, it powers players to take bigger situations to make up for the more prominent benefit capability of multi-day holds. On the other hand, it is ideal for decreasing position size when holding through numerous meetings to consider more noteworthy development and prevent situation further away from the current activity.

Profitable Exits

Leave when the cost is moving quickly into an overextended specialized state. This overextended state is frequently recognized by a progression of vertical bars on the hour-long graph. Then again, the cost could penetrate the third or fourth standard deviation of a top or base 20-day Bollinger Band.

Straighten out stops or consider a visually impaired leave when technical hindrances are strike like a significant trendline or past high/low. Exit or take halfway benefits when hybrids signal potential pattern changes.

Advantages of Momentum Investing

Momentum putting can transform into huge benefits for the dealer who has the correct character, deal with the dangers implied, and devote themselves to adhering to the strategy.

Potential for High Profits Over a Short Period

There are practical benefits to be produced using Momentum contribution. For instance, say you purchase a stock that develops from $50 to $75 dependent on an excessively sure investigator report. You, at that point, sell at a benefit of the half before the stock cost revises itself. You've made a half return throughout half a month or months (not an annualized return). After some time, the benefit potential increment utilizing Momentum contributing can be incredibly huge.

Utilizing the Market's Volatility to Your Advantage

The way to Momentum contributing has the option to exploit irregular market patterns. Momentum financial backers search for stocks to put resources into that are on their way up and afterwards sell them before the costs begin to return down. For such financial backers, being in front of the pack is an approach to expand profit from investment (ROI).

Utilizing the Emotional Decisions of Other Investors

As per Ben Carlson of the blog A Wealth of Common Sense, the whole thought of Momentum contributing is worked around pursuing execution. In any case, Momentum financial backers to do this efficiently that incorporates a particular purchasing point and selling point. Maybe then be constrained by passionate reactions to stock costs like numerous financial backers. Momentum financial backers look to exploit the progressions in stock costs brought about by enthusiastic financial backers.

Disadvantages of Momentum Investing

Notwithstanding, for each silver-lined cloud, there may likewise be a downpour. Momentum contributing additionally has a few disadvantages. A similar danger return tradeoff that exists with other putting techniques additionally plays a hand in Momentum contributing.

Like a boat attempting to cruise on the peaks of waves, a Momentum financial backer is consistently in danger of timing a purchase inaccurately and winding up submerged. Most Momentum financial backers acknowledge this danger as an instalment for the chance of more significant yields.

High Turnover

High stock turnover can be costly regarding expenses. Even though minimal effort representatives are gradually stopping high charges, this is as yet a significant worry for most newbie Momentum dealers.

Time Intensive

Momentum financial backers need to screen market subtleties day by day, if not hourly. Since they manage stocks that will peak and go down once more, they need to hop in ahead of schedule and get out quick. This implies observing every one of the updates to check whether there is any regrettable news that will frighten financial backers.

Market Sensitive

Momentum putting works best in a positively trending market since financial backers will, in the general group, significantly more. In a bear market, the edge for benefit on Momentum puts contracts per expanded financial backer alert.

Does it Work?

Just like the case with so numerous other contributing styles, the appropriate response is confounded. We should investigate.

Ransack Arnott, executive and organizer of Research Affiliates, investigated this inquiry, and this is the thing that he found. "No U.S. common asset with 'Momentum' in its name has, since its initiation, beated their benchmark net of charges and expenses."

Strangely, Arnott's exploration likewise showed that recreated portfolios that put a hypothetical Momentum contributing strategy to work really "add exceptional worth, in most time-frames and in most resource classes."8 However, when utilized in a real situation, the outcomes are poor. Why? In two words: exchanging costs. The entirety of that purchasing and selling works up a ton of business and commission expenses.

Dealers who cling to an Momentum strategy should be at the switch and prepared to purchase and sell consistently. Benefits work over months, not years. This is rather than basic purchase and-hold procedures that take a set it-and-fail to remember its approach.

For the individuals who take mid-day breaks or essentially don't have a premium in watching the market each day, there are Momentum-style trade-exchangeable assets (ETFs). These offers give a financial backer admittance to a bin of stocks considered normal for Momentum protection.

The Appeal of Momentum Investing

Despite a portion of its deficiencies, Momentum contributing has its allure. Consider, for instance, that "The MSCI World Momentum Index has arrived at the midpoint of yearly gains of 7.3% in the course of recent many years, double that of the more extensive benchmark." This return most likely doesn't represent exchanging costs and the time needed for execution.

Ongoing examination discovers it very well might be feasible to effectively exchange a Momentum strategy without the requirement for full-time exchanging and research. Utilizing U.S. information from the New York Stock Exchange (NYSE) somewhere in the range of 1991 and 2010, a recent report tracked down that an improved on Momentum strategy beat the benchmark even after representing exchange costs. Also, a base investment of $5,000 was sufficient to understand the benefits.9

A similar exploration found that contrasting this essential strategy with one of the more constant, more modest exchanges showed the last beat it, yet just to a certain extent. At some point or another, the exchanging expenses of a quickfire approach disintegrated the profits. Even better, the scientists discovered that "the ideal Momentum exchanging recurrence goes from bi-yearly to month to month"— a shockingly sensible pace.

Shorting

As referenced before, Momentumful Momentum brokers may utilize short selling to support their profits. This procedure permits a financial backer to benefit from a drop in a resource's cost. For instance, the quick vendor—accepting security will fall in price—gets

50 offers, adding up to $100. Then, the short merchant quickly sells those offers on the market for $100 and afterwards trusts that the resource will drop. At the point when it does, they repurchase the 50 offers (so they can be gotten back to the moneylender) at, suppose, $25. Subsequently, the short merchant acquired $100 on the underlying deal, at that point, burned through $25 to get the offers back for an addition of $75.

The issue with this strategy is that there is a limitless drawback hazard. In ordinary contributing, the drawback hazard is the absolute worth of your investment. On the off chance that you donate $100, the most you can lose is $100. In any case, with short selling, your greatest conceivable misfortune is boundless. In the situation above, for instance, you acquire 50 offers and sell them for $100. In any case, maybe the stock doesn't drop true to form. It goes up.

The 50 offers are valued at $150, at that point $200, etc. Eventually, the short merchant should repurchase the offers to return them to the bank. On the off chance that the offer cost continues to build, this will be a costly recommendation.

Strategy 4: Dollar-Cost Averaging

Dollar-cost averaging (DCA) is the act of making ordinary investments in the market over the long run and isn't fundamentally unrelated to different strategies depicted previously. Maybe, it is a method for executing whatever process you picked. With DCA, you may decide to put $300 in an investment account each month. This restrained methodology turns out to be especially amazing when you utilize mechanized highlights that contribute to you. It's not difficult to focus on an arrangement when the interaction requires no oversight.

The advantage of the DCA strategy is that it maintains a strategic distance from the agonizing and disastrous strategy of market timing. Indeed, even prepared financial backers sporadically feel the compulsion to purchase when they think costs are low to find. Regrettably, they have a more drawn out approach to drop.

When investments occur in standard additions, the financial backer catches costs at all levels, from high to low. These intermittent investments viably below the normal per share cost of the buys. Giving DCA something to do implies settling on three boundaries:

- The all-out whole to be contributed
- The window of time during which the investments will be made
- The recurrence of buys

A Wise Choice

Dollar-cost averaging is an intelligent decision for most financial backers. It keeps you focused on saving while at the same time lessening the degree of hazard and the impacts of unpredictability. However, for those in the situation to contribute a precise amount, DCA may not be the best methodology.

"By and large, we track down that a LSI (singular amount investment) approach has outflanked a DCA approach roughly 66% of the time, in any event, when results are adapted to the higher instability of a stock/bond portfolio versus cash investments."

However, most financial backers are not in a situation to make a solitary, enormous investment. Like this, DCA is proper for most. Besides, a DCA approach is a successful countermeasure to the intellectual predisposition innate to people. New and experienced financial backers the same are powerless to hard-wired imperfections in judgment. Misfortune repugnance predisposition, for instance, makes us see the increase or loss of a measure of money lopsidedly. Furthermore, affirmation inclination drives us to zero in on and recall data that affirms our since a long time ago held convictions while disregarding opposing data that might be significant.

Dollar-cost averaging goes around these normal issues by eliminating human frailties from the condition. Customary, mechanized investments forestall unconstrained, nonsensical conduct. A similar Vanguard study finished up, "If the financial backer is essentially worried about limiting disadvantage hazard and expected sensations of disappointment (coming about because of singular amount contributing preceding a market decline), at that point DCA might be of use."10

Once you've Identified Your Strategy

So you've limited a strategy. Fantastic! Be that as it may, there are as yet a couple of things you'll have to do before you put aside the initial instalment into your investment account.

To begin with, sort out how much money you need to cover your investments. That incorporates the amount you can store from the outset and the amount you can keep on contributing going ahead.

You'll, at that point, need to choose the ideal path for you to contribute. Do you plan to go to a conventional financial consultant or representative, or is an inactive, straightforward methodology more fitting for you? On the off chance that you pick the last mentioned, consider joining with a Robo consultant. This will help you sort out the cost of contributing from the board expenses to commissions you'll have to pay your dealer or counsellor. Something else to remember: Don't dismiss manager supported 401ks — that is an extraordinary method to begin contributing. Most organizations permit you to contribute part of your check and hide it tax-exempt, and many will coordinate with your commitments. You will not receive notification since you don't need to do a thing.

Think about your investment vehicles. Recollect that it doesn't assist with keeping your eggs in a single bin, so make sure you spread your money around to various investment vehicles by broadening—stocks, bonds, common assets, ETFs. In case you're socially conscious, you may think about capable of contributing. This is the ideal opportunity to sort out what you need your investment portfolio to be made of and what it will resemble.

Constructing a portfolio can likewise raise such intricacies as to how best to adjust the danger of certain investments against their expected returns. Consider finding support. Given innovation and the furious rivalry for your investments, more assets than any time in recent memory are accessible. Those alternatives incorporate Robo-consultants, remote helpers that can assist you with making a reasonable portfolio at a low cost, and charge just financial counsellors, who don't rely upon pay from commissions on the items they sell you. Put your exchanging abilities under serious scrutiny with our FREE Stock Simulator. Rival a great many Investopedia merchants and exchange your way to the top! Submit exchanges a virtual climate before you begin taking a chance with your own money. Work on exchanging systems so when you're prepared to enter the open market, you've had the training you need. The hardest piece of contributing is beginning, yet the sooner you do, the more you should make. That's all there is to it. Contributing can get muddled; however, the essentials are basic. Amplify the sum you save and your manager's commitments. Limit assessments and expenses. Settle on brilliant decisions with your restricted assets.

Constructing a portfolio can likewise raise such intricacies as to how best to adjust the danger of certain investments against their expected returns. Consider finding support. Given innovation and the furious rivalry for your investments, more assets than any time in recent memory are accessible. Those choices incorporate Robo-counselors, remote helpers that can assist you with making a decent portfolio at a low cost, and expense just financial consultants, who don't rely upon pay from commissions on the items they sell you. Put your exchanging abilities under a magnifying glass with our FREE

Stock Simulator. Contend with a large number of Investopedia brokers and exchange your way to the top! Submit exchanges a virtual climate before you begin taking a chance with your own money. Work on exchanging techniques so when you're prepared to enter the open market, you've had the training you need. The hardest piece of contributing is beginning; however, the sooner you do, the more you should make. That's all there is to it.

Contributing is an exciting ride, so keep your feelings under control. It might appear to be stunning when your investments are bringing in money, yet it could be hard to deal with when they assume a misfortune. That is the reason it's essential to make a stride back, remove your feelings from the condition and audit your investments with your guide consistently to ensure they're on target.

Get started investing as early as possible

Contributing when you're youthful is perhaps the most ideal approaches to see strong profits from your money. That is on account of compound profit, which implies your investment returns begin procuring their return. Compounding permits your record equilibrium to accelerate after some time.

How that functions, by and by: Let's say you contribute $200 consistently for a very long time and acquire a 6% normal yearly return. Toward the finish of the 10-year time frame, you'll have $33,300. Of that sum, $24,200 is money you've contributed — that $ 200 month to month commitments — and $9,100 is revenue you've procured on your investment.

There will be high points and low points in the stock market, obviously, however contributing youthful methods, you have a long time to brave them — and a very long time for your money to develop. Start now, regardless of whether you need to begin little.

If you're as yet unconvinced by the force of contributing, utilize our expansion adding machine to perceive how swelling can cut into your reserve funds if you don't contribute.

Decide how much to invest

The amount you ought to contribute relies upon your investment objective and when you need to arrive at it.

One common investment objective is retirement. On the off chance that you have a retirement account at work, similar to a 401(k), and it offers to coordinate with dollars, your first contributing achievement is simple: Contribute at any rate enough to that record to acquire the full match. That is free money, and you would prefer not to pass it up.

When in doubt of thumb, you need to mean to contribute an aggregate of 10% to 15% of your pay every year for retirement — your manager match checks toward that objective. That may sound ridiculous now; however, you can move gradually dependent upon it after some time.

For other contributing objectives, think about your time skyline and the sum you need; at that point, work in reverse to separate that sum into the month-to-month or week after week investments.

Open an investment account

If you don't have a 401(k), you can put for retirement in an individual retirement account, similar to a conventional or Roth IRA.

If you're contributing for another objective, you probably need to keep away from retirement accounts — which are intended to be utilized for retirement and subsequently have limitations about when and how you can take your money back out — and pick an available investment fund. You can eliminate money from a general investment fund whenever.

A typical misinterpretation is that you need a ton of money to open an investment account or begin contributing. That is just false. (We even have a guide for how to contribute $500.) Many online specialists, which offer the two IRAs and standard financier investment accounts, require no base investment to open a record. There are many assets accessible for moderately limited quantities.

Understand your investment options

Regardless of whether you contribute through a 401(k) or comparable boss supported retirement plan, in a customary or Roth IRA, or a standard investment account, you pick what to put resources into.

It's essential to see each instrument and how much danger it conveys. The most famous investments for those simply beginning include:

Stocks

A stock is a portion of proprietorship in a solitary organization. Stocks are otherwise called values.

Stocks are bought at an offer cost, going from the single digits a few thousand dollars, contingent upon the organization. We suggest buying stocks through shared assets, which we'll detail underneath.

Bonds

A bond is a credit to an organization or government element, which consents to take care of you in a specific number of years. Meanwhile, you get interested.

Bonds by and large are safer than stocks since you know precisely when you'll be repaid and the amount you'll procure. Be that as it may, bonds acquire lower long haul returns, so they should make up just a little piece of a drawn-out investment portfolio.

Mutual funds

A common asset is a combination of investments bundled as one. Common assets permit financial backers to skirt crafted by picking singular stocks and bonds and rather buy a different assortment in one exchange. The innate expansion of shared assets makes them, by and large, safer than distinct stocks.

An expert oversees some common assets, yet file reserves — a kind of shared asset — follow the presentation of a particular stock market file, similar to the S&P 500. By disposing of the expert administration, list reserves can charge lower expenses than effectively oversaw shared assets.

Most 401(k)s offer a curated determination of shared or record assets with no base investment, yet outside of those plans, these assets may require at least $1,000 or more.

Chapter 3: 10 Day Trading Strategies for Starters

Given below is a list of day trading strategies for the beginners.

- Knowledge Is The Main Thing
- Funds Are Set Aside
- Time Also Set Aside
- Start From Small
- Penny Stocks Avoiding
- Those Trades Should Be Timed
- Losses Are Cut By Orders Limit
- About Profits Be Realistic
- Stay Calm And Cool
- Follow The Plan

1. Knowledge Is the Main Thing

Besides knowing basic procedures of trading, day traders require to follow the latest events and news of the stock market affecting the stocks — economic outlook, plans interest rate from the Fed, etc. So, homework should be done. A wish list is created of securities you want to share to hold you up-to-date on general markets to selected companies. Scan news about the business and also visit reliable websites of financial.

2. Funds Are Set Aside

Evaluate the capital you are prepared to risk on every trade. A lot of day traders that are successful risk their account per trade from less than one percent to two percent. If a trading account of $40,000 you have and you are willing 0.5 percent risk of the capital of yours on every trade, your loss maximum is 200 dollars (0.5 percent * $40,000) per trade. A surplus is set aside the sum of funds for which you can exchange and you're able to fail. Remember, it can happen or it may not.

3. Time Also Set Aside

The trading day requires your attention. That's why they name it day trading. In reality you'll have to give much of the day. If a little time to spend you have, don't do it. In this process a trader needs to track markets and spot the available opportunities that may arise during hours of trading, any time. Rapid movement is essential.

4. Start From Small

As a starter, focus during a session on a maximum of 1-2 inventories. With only a few inventories, tracking the markets and finding the opportunities is a lot easier. Recently, trading fractional shares have become common increasingly, so smaller specific amounts of dollars can be specified by you for investing. That means if shares of Apple at $250 are trading and you just want $50 worth to buy, many brokers now will let you buy a share of one-fifth.

5. Penny Stocks Avoiding

You will want sales and cheap rates so from penny stocks keep away. Often illiquid these stocks are and there are often bleak chances of the jackpot hit. Most trading of stocks below a share of $5 are removed from the list from global stock markets and are now OTC (over-counter) tradable Keep out of these unless a genuine chance is seen by you and the work is one.

6. Those Trades Should Be Timed

A lot of orders issued by traders and investors start executing as the morning markets begin, which leads to the volatility of the price. A player of the season can identify trends and choose suitably to make money. But for beginners, it's better to read the market only without any moves for the start, 15-20 mins. The hours in the middle are less volatile usually, and after that move toward the closing bell begins to rise again.

Even though the opportunities are offered by the rush hours, at first it is safe for the starter to avoid these.

7. Losses Are Cut By Orders Limit

Many orders issued by Decide what kind of orders you can need for trades entering and exiting. Will you respond to business requests or filter requests?

It is performed at the highest price possible at the moment that you put a business

Order — thus, no quality guarantee. A maximum order, however, promises not the execution but the demand. Orders limit allow you to exchange more efficiently, whereby you set the price (not unreasonable but executable) on both selling and buying.

More experienced and sophisticated day traders might use strategies of options to hedge positions of theirs also.

8. About Profits Be Realistic

A plan should not succeed to be successful every time. Many traders earn just 50 percent to 60 percent of their companies. They do make better on their champions, though, than on their losers they lose. Making sure that the liability with each exchange is restricted to the account single amount, and that methods of entering and exit are well written down and specified.

9. Stay Calm and Cool

During moments that financial markets are checking the emotions. Yo u require to learn, to keep fear, hope, and greed at bay.

On facts decisions can be focused and not on feelings.

10. Follow the Plan

Traders that are successful need to move quickly but they do not need to think quickly. Why? For what? Because in advance a trading strategy is developed by them, along with that strategy sticking discipline. It's important to be closely following your formula rather than trying profit chasing. Do not let your feelings get the better out from you and give up the plan. Between day traders there is a mantra: "Plan the trade and trade the plan of yours."Before going in the day trading details, let's have a look at a few reasons why so difficult is the day trading.

Why Difficult is the Day Trading?

It requires very much practice and knowhow and several factors are there that might make the process difficult. Know firstly that against the professionals you are going whose life majorly around trading revolves. Such individuals have exposure to the industry's latest technologies and networks and they are made to win eventually even though they struggle. If upon the bandwagon you jump, that ensures they can get more money.

No matter, tax reduction how much slim, would be a fall in your earnings.

Note, taxes are going to be paid by you at the rate of annual of any gains of short-term — including other assets that you keep for a year or longer. The only drawback is that all profits will outweigh the losses. You can be susceptible to cognitive and psychological prejudices, as an individual investor. Professional traders usually can cut out these of their strategies of trading, but it is when involving your capital, a different side of the story it can be.

2.1 Taking Right Decision of What & When to Buy

Day traders aim to earn money through manipulating minute fluctuati ons in markets ofparticularassets (futures, currencies, stocks, and options), typically using vast quantities of capital for this.

In determining what to concentrate on, say in a warehouse, a day tra der typically searches for 3 things:

Liquidity, helps you to reach and leave a market at a reasonable price for example, spreads large, or the gap between the asking price and the bid, and slippage low, or the gap between a trade 's anticipated price and the price in real.

Volatility is just the price range expected daily measure— the range that operates a day trader within. Further uncertainty implies gain or lose. Trading frequency is a calculation of time a product is acquired and exchanged over a particular amount of time — most generally referred to as the actual average rate of exchange.

A high-volume degree indicates a considerable stock interest. A rise in the quantity of a stock is also an indicator of a market change, either upwards or downwards.

When you decide the stocks kind (or assets) you are searching for, you have to learn the entry points are identified how — at what specific moment you can invest.

Tools of help to you are:

News services Real-time: News changes markets, so subscribing to utilities that inform you what possibly market-driven news is coming out is vital.

Electronic Communications Networks/Level II quotes: ECNs are systems computer-based that show the best bid available and request quotations from various participants of the market, and then coordinate and orders are executed automatically. Level II is a service subscription-based that offers real-time exposure to the

stock market order book consisting of demand quotations from makers of the market reporting through stock market mentioned and protection from the Bulletin Board OTC. Together they will send you a feeling of real-time orders being performed.

2.2 Charts Regarding Intraday Candlestick:

Candlestick gives a direct price-acting analysis.

Much later on those. Specify the requirements in which you must reach a role, and write them down. "Purchase during uptrend" is not very precise. Anything like it is even more precise and even testable: "Invest on the two-minute chart in the first two hours of the trading day when the price breaks over the upper trend of a sequence of the triangle, the triangle where was followed by an upward trend (one higher high swing and higher low swing at least before the formation of the triangle)."

If a clear collection you have of entry laws, search more charts thoroughly to look if certain requirements are produced every
day (if you want every day, day trade) and often more than not deliver a price change in the direction predicted.
If so, a potentially valuable entry point you have. You would then have to decide whether to leave, or offer, certain trades.

When to Sell Decision

There are many ways to leave a winning place, like profit targets   and stops trailing.

Plan	Explanation
Scalping	It is the most commonly employed techniques.

	Selling It involves after a profitable trade becomes, almost immediately. The price goal is something which translates to "money had been made by you on this offer."
Fading	Fading, after rapid upward movement, includes stocks shorting. This is focused on the premise that (1)overbought, (2) st art buyers are likely to continue profit- taking, and (3) current buyers might be frightened. This technique can be incredibly satisfying though dange rous. The price goal here is when investors start again coming back.
Daily Pivots	This involves capitalizing on the daily volatility of a stock. This is achieved by purchasing attempts at a day 's small and sell heavy at a day. The target of the price here is at the upcoming sign of a setback simply.
Momentu m	It involves trading usually on the release of news or finding powerful, high volume-supported trending moves. On news releases one form of the trader of momentum can purchase and a pattern is ridden before it shows reversal signs. The other price surge type will fade. Quality goal here is when the amount begins to decline.

This strategy most of the time, you will want an asset exit when stock interest decreases as shown by ECN / level II and volume. The target of the profit should allow also extra profit on winning businesses to be made then on losing businesses lost. If the stop-loss is 0.05 dollars away from the entrance point, it will be more than 0.05 dollars away from your goal.

Defines just how you can leave your trades when you reach them, much as your entry stage. The exit requirements ought to be fairly precise to be testable and repeatable.
Typically means betting on press reports or having solid discoveries.

2.3 Techniques Of Losses Limiting During Day Trading

An order of stop-loss is intended to limit the losses on a security position.
stop-loss may be put under a low recently for the long position, or above high recently for the short positions. It can also be volatile based.
E.g., if a price of the stock moves around 0.05 dollars a min, then might you can put a $0.15 stop loss away from the entry to allow some space to the price to fluctuate until in the direction it moves you expect. Defines exactly how you are going to control the trade risks.
E.g., in the triangle trend case, if purchasing a breakdown, stop
loss may be put 0.02 dollars below a swing low recently, or 0.02 dollars below the trend.
(The 0.02 dollars is arbitrary.)
2 stop losses set is one of the strategies:

1. A specific order of stop-loss imposed at a particular amount of quality that fits the risk perception. That is basically the most wealth that you can afford to waste.

2. A visual stop-loss installed at the stage that it fails the entry requirements. This ensures you will be leaving your place instantly if an abrupt switch is taken by the trade. The exit conditions must be

clear enough to be repeatable and testable and, if you want to leave the trades. Also, establishing a per day maximum loss that you can manage to withstand — psychologically and financially both is crucial. Just take rest for the day whenever you hit this point. Keep to the perimeters and prepare. Tomorrow, after all, is just another (trade) day.

You will decide how the future approach suits under the risk cap after you have established how you join trades and the stop loss can where to be positioned. If the approach is leading you to so much danger, you must adjust the plan to that the danger in any way. If the technique falls below the risk limit of your then research should start. To locate your entries through historical maps go manually, indicating whether the stop failure or goal should have been reached. By this, paper trading for 50 trades to 100 trades at least, noting if the profitable was the strategy and also if it meets the expectations of yours.

If it meets, then move to trade in real-time the strategy (demo account). If it is successful in a virtual world over the period of two or more months, continue on with the technique of day trading with real money. If a strategy doesn't make a profit, start over.

Remember that if margin trading — which means you borrow from a brokerage company the investment funds of yours (and remember that for day trading there are high margin requirements)—you are far more at risk to sharp movements of the price. Margin helps amplify the results of trading not only by profit but also by losses if against you the trade goes.

Hence, the use is crucial to stop losses when trading marginally on a day. Now, understanding few days trading details, let's have a glance at some main tactics that novice day traders may use.

2.4 Basic Strategies of Day Trading

If you have learned few methods, established your own unique types of trading and decided what your objectives are, you will use a set of t actics to support you in the search for money.

Here are a few common technique that   can be   used   by you. While few of these above   listed, worth looking back into they are:

- Tracking the pattern: Whoever observes the pattern can purchase as rates go up or sell short when they go down. This is based under the premise that rates which have gradually increased or decreased will tend so.
- Different investment: This plan predicts price increases can plunge and reverse. At the increase buys the contrarian during the decline or sell short, with the explicit hope that the pattern will shift.
- Scalping: It is a method in which the speculator utilizes minor market holes generated by the distribution of the asking bid. Normally this technique involves rapid entry and exit of a position — in mins or even secs.
- News trading: this strategy user investor will invest when some good news is there or selling short when bad news arises.

That will contribute to more uncertainty, which

can result in higher gains or losses.

Trading on the Day is hard to learn. It calls for energy, discipline, and skills. Many that attempt it struggle but the above-mentioned strategies and guidance will help you build a successful approach. You will significantly increase the likelihood of overcoming odds with adequate   preparation   and   regular   success   appraisal.

Conclusion

Putting away money may appear to be threatening, particularly on the off chance that you've never done it. In any case, if you sort out how you need to contribute, how much money you ought to contribute, and your danger resistance, you'll be all around situated to make savvy choices with your money that will work well for you for quite a long time to come. As should be obvious, a few kinds of investment systems take into account pretty much every degree of hazard, inclusion, and timing. Tracking down the best strategy for you will boil down to understanding your inclinations and financial circumstance. The best thing I can prescribe is to do your examination — what turns out incredible for a companion may not work for you. There is a great deal influencing everything regarding contributing, however with the correct assurance, you can discover a strategy that supports your financial wellbeing and assists you with accomplishing your objectives. Your investment strategy relies upon your saving objectives, how much money you need to contact them and your time skyline.

On the off chance that your reserve funds objective is over 20 years away (like retirement), practically the entirety of your money can be in stocks. Be that as it may, picking explicit stocks can be muddled and tedious, so for the vast majority, the ideal approach to put resources into stocks is through minimal effort stock common assets, record assets or ETFs.

Suppose you're putting something aside for a short objective, and you need the money inside five years. In that case, the danger related to stocks implies you're in an ideal situation protecting your money, in an online investment account, cash the executive's record or okay investment portfolio. We layout the perfect choices for transient reserve funds here.

If you can't or don't have any desire to conclude, you can open an investment account (counting an IRA) through a robo-counsellor, an investment the executive's administration utilizes PC calculations to fabricate and take care of your investment portfolio.

Robo-counsels generally assemble their portfolios out of minimal effort ETFs and list reserves. Since they offer low costs and low or no essentials, robos let you begin rapidly. They charge a little expense for a portfolio on the board, by and large, around 0.25% of your record balance. Contributing can get muddled, yet the essentials are straightforward. Amplify the sum you save and your manager's commitments. Limit assessments and charges. Settle on wise decisions with your restricted assets.

Lightning Source UK Ltd.
Milton Keynes UK
UKHW022037280521
384576UK00002B/243